THIS GREAT ENGLISH CAMPER VAN TRAVEL JOURNAL

BELONGS TO

Name ....

E MAIL ....

MOBILE ....

BLOG ....

PLEASE RETURN IF FOUND

CAMPER VAN TRAVEL JOURNAL

DATE .... MILEAGE START ....
DEPARTURE TIME .... MILEAGE END ....
ARRIVAL TIME .... MILEAGE TOTAL ....

CAMPSITE NAME ....
ADDRESS 1 ....
ADDRESS 2 ....
POST CODE .... GPS ....
E MAIL .... PHONE ....
WEBSITE WWW..
MY RATING ☆☆☆☆☆☆☆☆   RECOMMEND YES/NO
WEATHER .... TEMPERATURE ....

WILD CAMPING LOCATION/ NOTES

....
....
....
.... GPS ....

DAILY COSTS		TODAY'S HIGHLIGHTS
SITE FEES	£ .	....
FUEL	£ .	....
LPG GAS	£ .	....
TOLLS	£ .	....
GROCERIES	£ .	....
EATING OUT	£ .	....
ENTERTAINMENT	£ .	....
OTHER COSTS	£ .	....

NOTES

....
....
....
....

CAMPER VAN TRAVEL JOURNAL

DATE .... MILEAGE START ....
DEPARTURE TIME .... MILEAGE END ....
ARRIVAL TIME .... MILEAGE TOTAL ....

CAMPSITE NAME ....
ADDRESS 1 ....
ADDRESS 2 ....
POST CODE .... GPS ....
E MAIL .... PHONE ....
WEBSITE WWW...
MY RATING ☆☆☆☆☆☆☆   RECOMMEND YES/NO
WEATHER .... TEMPERATURE ....

WILD CAMPING LOCATION/ NOTES

....
....
....
....
.... GPS ....

DAILY COSTS		TODAY'S HIGHLIGHTS
SITE FEES	£ .	....
FUEL	£ .	....
LPG GAS	£ .	....
TOLLS	£ .	....
GROCERIES	£ .	....
EATING OUT	£ .	....
ENTERTAINMENT	£ .	....
OTHER COSTS	£ .	....

NOTES

....
....
....
....
....

CAMPER VAN TRAVEL JOURNAL

DATE .... MILEAGE START ....
DEPARTURE TIME .... MILEAGE END ....
ARRIVAL TIME .... MILEAGE TOTAL ....

CAMPSITE NAME ....
ADDRESS 1 ....
ADDRESS 2 ....
POST CODE .... GPS ....
E MAIL .... PHONE ....
WEBSITE WWW...
MY RATING ☆☆☆☆☆☆☆☆☆   RECOMMEND YES/NO
WEATHER .... TEMPERATURE ....

WILD CAMPING LOCATION/ NOTES

....
....
....
.... GPS ....

DAILY COSTS	TODAY'S HIGHLIGHTS
SITE FEES £ .	....
FUEL £ .	....
LPG GAS £ .	....
TOLLS £ .	....
GROCERIES £ .	....
EATING OUT £ .	....
ENTERTAINMENT £ .	....
OTHER COSTS £ .	....

NOTES

....
....
....
....

CAMPER VAN TRAVEL JOURNAL

DATE .... MILEAGE START ....
DEPARTURE TIME .... MILEAGE END ....
ARRIVAL TIME .... MILEAGE TOTAL ....

CAMPSITE NAME ....
ADDRESS 1 ....
ADDRESS 2 ....
POST CODE .... GPS ....
E MAIL .... PHONE ....
WEBSITE WWW...
MY RATING ☆☆☆☆☆☆☆☆☆☆   RECOMMEND YES/NO
WEATHER .... TEMPERATURE ....

WILD CAMPING LOCATION/ NOTES

....
....
....
....
.... GPS ....

DAILY COSTS		TODAY'S HIGHLIGHTS
SITE FEES	£ .	....
FUEL	£ .	....
LPG GAS	£ .	....
TOLLS	£ .	....
GROCERIES	£ .	....
EATING OUT	£ .	....
ENTERTAINMENT	£ .	....
OTHER COSTS	£ .	....

NOTES

....
....
....
....

CAMPER VAN TRAVEL JOURNAL

DATE .... MILEAGE START ....
DEPARTURE TIME .... MILEAGE END ....
ARRIVAL TIME   .... MILEAGE TOTAL ....

CAMPSITE NAME ....
ADDRESS 1 ....
ADDRESS 2 ....
POST CODE .... GPS ....
E MAIL .... PHONE ....
WEBSITE WWW...
MY RATING ☆☆☆☆☆☆☆☆   RECOMMEND YES/NO
WEATHER .... TEMPERATURE ....

WILD CAMPING LOCATION/ NOTES

....
....
....
....
.... GPS ....

DAILY COSTS		TODAY'S HIGHLIGHTS
SITE FEES	£ .	....
FUEL	£ .	....
LPG GAS	£ .	....
TOLLS	£ .	....
GROCERIES	£ .	....
EATING OUT	£ .	....
ENTERTAINMENT	£ .	....
OTHER COSTS	£ .	....

NOTES

....
....
....
....
....

CAMPER VAN TRAVEL JOURNAL

DATE .... MILEAGE START ....
DEPARTURE TIME .... MILEAGE END ....
ARRIVAL TIME .... MILEAGE TOTAL ....

CAMPSITE NAME ....
ADDRESS 1 ....
ADDRESS 2 ....
POST CODE .... GPS ....
E MAIL .... PHONE ....
WEBSITE WWW...
MY RATING ☆☆☆☆☆☆☆☆   RECOMMEND YES/NO
WEATHER .... TEMPERATURE ....

WILD CAMPING LOCATION/ NOTES

....
....
....
....
.... GPS ....

DAILY COSTS		TODAY'S HIGHLIGHTS
SITE FEES	£ .	....
FUEL	£ .	....
LPG GAS	£ .	....
TOLLS	£ .	....
GROCERIES	£ .	....
EATING OUT	£ .	....
ENTERTAINMENT	£ .	....
OTHER COSTS	£ .	....

NOTES

....
....
....
....
....

CAMPER VAN TRAVEL JOURNAL

DATE .... MILEAGE START ....
DEPARTURE TIME .... MILEAGE END ....
ARRIVAL TIME .... MILEAGE TOTAL ....

CAMPSITE NAME ....
ADDRESS 1 ....
ADDRESS 2 ....
POST CODE .... GPS ....
E MAIL .... PHONE ....
WEBSITE WWW...
MY RATING ☆☆☆☆☆☆☆☆   RECOMMEND YES/NO
WEATHER .... TEMPERATURE ....

WILD CAMPING LOCATION/ NOTES

....
....
....
....
............................GPS ....

DAILY COSTS	TODAY'S HIGHLIGHTS
SITE FEES £ .	....
FUEL £ .	....
LPG GAS £ .	....
TOLLS £ .	....
GROCERIES £ .	....
EATING OUT £ .	....
ENTERTAINMENT £ .	....
OTHER COSTS £ .	....

NOTES

....
....
....
....
....

CAMPER VAN TRAVEL JOURNAL

DATE .... MILEAGE START ....
DEPARTURE TIME .... MILEAGE END ....
ARRIVAL TIME .... MILEAGE TOTAL ....

CAMPSITE NAME ....
ADDRESS 1 ....
ADDRESS 2 ....
POST CODE .... GPS ....
E MAIL .... PHONE ....
WEBSITE WWW ....
MY RATING ☆☆☆☆☆☆☆☆   RECOMMEND YES/NO
WEATHER .... TEMPERATURE ....

WILD CAMPING LOCATION/ NOTES

....
....
....
....
.... GPS ....

DAILY COSTS		TODAY'S HIGHLIGHTS
SITE FEES	£ .	....
FUEL	£ .	....
LPG GAS	£ .	....
TOLLS	£ .	....
GROCERIES	£ .	....
EATING OUT	£ .	....
ENTERTAINMENT	£ .	....
OTHER COSTS	£ .	....

NOTES

....
....
....
....
....

CAMPER VAN TRAVEL JOURNAL

DATE .... MILEAGE START ....
DEPARTURE TIME .... MILEAGE END ....
ARRIVAL TIME .... MILEAGE TOTAL ....

CAMPSITE NAME ....
ADDRESS 1 ....
ADDRESS 2 ....
POST CODE .... GPS ....
E MAIL .... PHONE ....
WEBSITE WWW...
MY RATING ☆☆☆☆☆☆☆   RECOMMEND YES/NO
WEATHER .... TEMPERATURE ....

WILD CAMPING LOCATION/ NOTES

....
....
....
.... GPS ....

DAILY COSTS		TODAY'S HIGHLIGHTS
SITE FEES	£ .	....
FUEL	£ .	....
LPG GAS	£ .	....
TOLLS	£ .	....
GROCERIES	£ .	....
EATING OUT	£ .	....
ENTERTAINMENT	£ .	....
OTHER COSTS	£ .	....

NOTES

....
....
....
....
....

CAMPER VAN TRAVEL JOURNAL

DATE .... MILEAGE START ....
DEPARTURE TIME .... MILEAGE END ....
ARRIVAL TIME .... MILEAGE TOTAL ....

CAMPSITE NAME ....
ADDRESS 1 ....
ADDRESS 2 ....
POST CODE .... GPS ....
E MAIL .... PHONE ....
WEBSITE WWW...
MY RATING ☆☆☆☆☆☆☆☆☆☆   RECOMMEND YES/NO
WEATHER .... TEMPERATURE ....

WILD CAMPING LOCATION/ NOTES
....
....
....
....
.... GPS ....

DAILY COSTS		TODAY'S HIGHLIGHTS
SITE FEES	£ .	....
FUEL	£ .	....
LPG GAS	£ .	....
TOLLS	£ .	....
GROCERIES	£ .	....
EATING OUT	£ .	....
ENTERTAINMENT	£ .	....
OTHER COSTS	£ .	....

NOTES
....
....
....
....

CAMPER VAN TRAVEL JOURNAL

DATE .... MILEAGE START ....
DEPARTURE TIME .... MILEAGE END ....
ARRIVAL TIME .... MILEAGE TOTAL ....

CAMPSITE NAME ....
ADDRESS 1 ....
ADDRESS 2 ....
POST CODE .... GPS ....
E MAIL .... PHONE ....
WEBSITE WWW..
MY RATING ☆☆☆☆☆☆☆   RECOMMEND YES/NO
WEATHER .... TEMPERATURE ....

WILD CAMPING LOCATION/ NOTES

....
....
....
....
.... GPS ....

DAILY COSTS		TODAY'S HIGHLIGHTS
SITE FEES	£ .	....
FUEL	£ .	....
LPG GAS	£ .	....
TOLLS	£ .	....
GROCERIES	£ .	....
EATING OUT	£ .	....
ENTERTAINMENT	£ .	....
OTHER COSTS	£ .	....

NOTES

....
....
....
....
....

CAMPER VAN TRAVEL JOURNAL

DATE .... MILEAGE START ....
DEPARTURE TIME .... MILEAGE END ....
ARRIVAL TIME .... MILEAGE TOTAL ....

CAMPSITE NAME ....
ADDRESS 1 ....
ADDRESS 2 ....
POST CODE .... GPS ....
E MAIL .... PHONE ....
WEBSITE WWW..
MY RATING ☆☆☆☆☆☆☆☆   RECOMMEND YES/NO
WEATHER .... TEMPERATURE ....

WILD CAMPING LOCATION/ NOTES

....
....
....
....
.... GPS ....

DAILY COSTS			TODAY'S HIGHLIGHTS
SITE FEES	£	.	....
FUEL	£	.	....
LPG GAS	£	.	....
TOLLS	£	.	....
GROCERIES	£	.	....
EATING OUT	£	.	....
ENTERTAINMENT	£	.	....
OTHER COSTS	£	.	....

NOTES

....
....
....
....
....

CAMPER VAN TRAVEL JOURNAL

DATE .... MILEAGE START ....
DEPARTURE TIME .... MILEAGE END ....
ARRIVAL TIME .... MILEAGE TOTAL ....

CAMPSITE NAME ....
ADDRESS 1 ....
ADDRESS 2 ....
POST CODE .... GPS ....
E MAIL .... PHONE ....
WEBSITE WWW...
MY RATING ☆☆☆☆☆☆☆☆   RECOMMEND YES/NO
WEATHER .... TEMPERATURE ....

WILD CAMPING LOCATION/ NOTES

....
....
....
....
.... GPS ....

DAILY COSTS	TODAY'S HIGHLIGHTS
SITE FEES £ .	....
FUEL £ .	....
LPG GAS £ .	....
TOLLS £ .	....
GROCERIES £ .	....
EATING OUT £ .	....
ENTERTAINMENT £ .	....
OTHER COSTS £ .	....

NOTES

....
....
....
....
....

CAMPER VAN TRAVEL JOURNAL

DATE .... MILEAGE START ....
DEPARTURE TIME .... MILEAGE END ....
ARRIVAL TIME .... MILEAGE TOTAL ....

CAMPSITE NAME ....
ADDRESS 1 ....
ADDRESS 2 ....
POST CODE .... GPS ....
E MAIL .... PHONE ....
WEBSITE WWW..
MY RATING ☆☆☆☆☆☆☆☆☆☆   RECOMMEND YES/NO
WEATHER .... TEMPERATURE ....

WILD CAMPING LOCATION/ NOTES

....
....
....
....
.... GPS ....

DAILY COSTS		TODAY'S HIGHLIGHTS
SITE FEES	£ .	....
FUEL	£ .	....
LPG GAS	£ .	....
TOLLS	£ .	....
GROCERIES	£ .	....
EATING OUT	£ .	....
ENTERTAINMENT	£ .	....
OTHER COSTS	£ .	....

NOTES

....
....
....
....
....

CAMPER VAN TRAVEL JOURNAL

DATE .... MILEAGE START ....
DEPARTURE TIME .... MILEAGE END ....
ARRIVAL TIME .... MILEAGE TOTAL ....

CAMPSITE NAME ....
ADDRESS 1 ....
ADDRESS 2 ....
POST CODE .... GPS ....
E MAIL .... PHONE ....
WEBSITE WWW..
MY RATING ☆☆☆☆☆☆☆☆   RECOMMEND YES/NO
WEATHER .... TEMPERATURE ....

WILD CAMPING LOCATION/ NOTES

....
....
....
....
.... GPS ....

DAILY COSTS	TODAY'S HIGHLIGHTS
SITE FEES £ .	....
FUEL £ .	....
LPG GAS £ .	....
TOLLS £ .	....
GROCERIES £ .	....
EATING OUT £ .	....
ENTERTAINMENT £ .	....
OTHER COSTS £ .	....

NOTES

....
....
....
....
....

CAMPER VAN TRAVEL JOURNAL

DATE .... MILEAGE START ....
DEPARTURE TIME .... MILEAGE END ....
ARRIVAL TIME .... MILEAGE TOTAL ....

CAMPSITE NAME ....
ADDRESS 1 ....
ADDRESS 2 ....
POST CODE .... GPS ....
E MAIL .... PHONE ....
WEBSITE WWW...
MY RATING ☆☆☆☆☆☆☆☆☆☆   RECOMMEND YES/NO
WEATHER .... TEMPERATURE ....

WILD CAMPING LOCATION/ NOTES

....
....
....
....
.... GPS ....

DAILY COSTS		TODAY'S HIGHLIGHTS
SITE FEES	£ .	....
FUEL	£ .	....
LPG GAS	£ .	....
TOLLS	£ .	....
GROCERIES	£ .	....
EATING OUT	£ .	....
ENTERTAINMENT	£ .	....
OTHER COSTS	£ .	....

NOTES

....
....
....
....
....

CAMPER VAN TRAVEL JOURNAL

DATE .... MILEAGE START ....
DEPARTURE TIME .... MILEAGE END ....
ARRIVAL TIME .... MILEAGE TOTAL ....

CAMPSITE NAME ....
ADDRESS 1 ....
ADDRESS 2 ....
POST CODE .... GPS ....
E MAIL .... PHONE ....
WEBSITE WWW...
MY RATING ☆ ☆ ☆ ☆ ☆ ☆ ☆   RECOMMEND YES/NO
WEATHER .... TEMPERATURE ....

WILD CAMPING LOCATION/ NOTES

....
....
....
....
.... GPS ....

DAILY COSTS		TODAY'S HIGHLIGHTS
SITE FEES	£ .	....
FUEL	£ .	....
LPG GAS	£ .	....
TOLLS	£ .	....
GROCERIES	£ .	....
EATING OUT	£ .	....
ENTERTAINMENT	£ .	....
OTHER COSTS	£ .	....

NOTES

....
....
....
....
....

CAMPER VAN TRAVEL JOURNAL

DATE .... MILEAGE START ....
DEPARTURE TIME .... MILEAGE END ....
ARRIVAL TIME .... MILEAGE TOTAL ....

CAMPSITE NAME ....
ADDRESS 1 ....
ADDRESS 2 ....
POST CODE .... GPS ....
E MAIL .... PHONE ....
WEBSITE WWW...
MY RATING ☆☆☆☆☆☆☆☆☆☆   RECOMMEND YES/NO
WEATHER .... TEMPERATURE ....

WILD CAMPING LOCATION/ NOTES

....
....
....
....
.... GPS ....

DAILY COSTS		TODAY'S HIGHLIGHTS
SITE FEES	£ .	....
FUEL	£ .	....
LPG GAS	£ .	....
TOLLS	£ .	....
GROCERIES	£ .	....
EATING OUT	£ .	....
ENTERTAINMENT	£ .	....
OTHER COSTS	£ .	....

NOTES

....
....
....
....

CAMPER VAN TRAVEL JOURNAL

DATE .... MILEAGE START ....
DEPARTURE TIME .... MILEAGE END ....
ARRIVAL TIME .... MILEAGE TOTAL ....

CAMPSITE NAME ....
ADDRESS 1 ....
ADDRESS 2 ....
POST CODE .... GPS ....
E MAIL .... PHONE ....
WEBSITE WWW..
MY RATING ☆☆☆☆☆☆☆☆☆   RECOMMEND YES/NO
WEATHER .... TEMPERATURE ....

WILD CAMPING LOCATION/ NOTES

....
....
....
....
.... GPS ....

DAILY COSTS	TODAY'S HIGHLIGHTS
SITE FEES £ .	....
FUEL £ .	....
LPG GAS £ .	....
TOLLS £ .	....
GROCERIES £ .	....
EATING OUT £ .	....
ENTERTAINMENT £ .	....
OTHER COSTS £ .	....

NOTES

....
....
....
....
....

CAMPER VAN TRAVEL JOURNAL

DATE .... MILEAGE START ....
DEPARTURE TIME .... MILEAGE END ....
ARRIVAL TIME .... MILEAGE TOTAL ....

CAMPSITE NAME ....
ADDRESS 1 ....
ADDRESS 2 ....
POST CODE .... GPS ....
E MAIL .... PHONE ....
WEBSITE WWW...
MY RATING ☆☆☆☆☆☆☆   RECOMMEND YES/NO
WEATHER .... TEMPERATURE ....

WILD CAMPING LOCATION/ NOTES

....
....
....
....
.... GPS ....

DAILY COSTS		TODAY'S HIGHLIGHTS
SITE FEES	£ .	....
FUEL	£ .	....
LPG GAS	£ .	....
TOLLS	£ .	....
GROCERIES	£ .	....
EATING OUT	£ .	....
ENTERTAINMENT	£ .	....
OTHER COSTS	£ .	....

NOTES

....
....
....
....
....

CAMPER VAN TRAVEL JOURNAL

DATE .... MILEAGE START ....
DEPARTURE TIME .... MILEAGE END ....
ARRIVAL TIME .... MILEAGE TOTAL ....

CAMPSITE NAME ....
ADDRESS 1 ....
ADDRESS 2 ....
POST CODE .... GPS ....
E MAIL .... PHONE ....
WEBSITE WWW..
MY RATING ☆☆☆☆☆☆☆   RECOMMEND YES/NO
WEATHER .... TEMPERATURE ....

WILD CAMPING LOCATION/ NOTES

....
....
....
....
.... GPS ....

DAILY COSTS	TODAY'S HIGHLIGHTS
SITE FEES £ .	....
FUEL £ .	....
LPG GAS £ .	....
TOLLS £ .	....
GROCERIES £ .	....
EATING OUT £ .	....
ENTERTAINMENT £ .	....
OTHER COSTS £ .	....

NOTES

....
....
....
....
....

CAMPER VAN TRAVEL JOURNAL

DATE .... MILEAGE START ....
DEPARTURE TIME............ MILEAGE END ....
ARRIVAL TIME   .... MILEAGE TOTAL ....

CAMPSITE NAME ....
ADDRESS 1 ....
ADDRESS 2 ....
POST CODE .... GPS ....
E MAIL .... PHONE ....
WEBSITE WWW...
MY RATING ☆☆☆☆☆☆☆   RECOMMEND YES/NO
WEATHER .... TEMPERATURE ....

WILD CAMPING LOCATION/ NOTES
....
....
....
....
.... GPS ....

DAILY COSTS	TODAY'S HIGHLIGHTS
SITE FEES £ .	....
FUEL £ .	....
LPG GAS £ .	....
TOLLS £ .	....
GROCERIES £ .	....
EATING OUT £ .	....
ENTERTAINMENT £ .	....
OTHER COSTS £ .	....

NOTES
....
....
....
....
....

CAMPER VAN TRAVEL JOURNAL

DATE .... MILEAGE START ....
DEPARTURE TIME .... MILEAGE END ....
ARRIVAL TIME .... MILEAGE TOTAL ....

CAMPSITE NAME ....
ADDRESS 1 ....
ADDRESS 2 ....
POST CODE .... GPS ....
E MAIL .... PHONE ....
WEBSITE WWW..
MY RATING ☆☆☆☆☆☆☆☆   RECOMMEND YES/NO
WEATHER .... TEMPERATURE ....

WILD CAMPING LOCATION/ NOTES

....
....
....
.... GPS ....

DAILY COSTS		TODAY'S HIGHLIGHTS
SITE FEES	£ .	....
FUEL	£ .	....
LPG GAS	£ .	....
TOLLS	£ .	....
GROCERIES	£ .	....
EATING OUT	£ .	....
ENTERTAINMENT	£ .	....
OTHER COSTS	£ .	....

NOTES

....
....
....
....
....

CAMPER VAN TRAVEL JOURNAL

DATE .... MILEAGE START ....
DEPARTURE TIME .... MILEAGE END ....
ARRIVAL TIME .... MILEAGE TOTAL ....

CAMPSITE NAME ....
ADDRESS 1 ....
ADDRESS 2 ....
POST CODE .... GPS ....
E MAIL .... PHONE ....
WEBSITE WWW...
MY RATING ☆☆☆☆☆☆☆☆☆☆   RECOMMEND YES/NO
WEATHER .... TEMPERATURE ....

WILD CAMPING LOCATION/ NOTES

....
....
....
....
.... GPS ....

DAILY COSTS		TODAY'S HIGHLIGHTS
SITE FEES	£ .	....
FUEL	£ .	....
LPG GAS	£ .	....
TOLLS	£ .	....
GROCERIES	£ .	....
EATING OUT	£ .	....
ENTERTAINMENT	£ .	....
OTHER COSTS	£ .	....

NOTES

....
....
....
....
....

CAMPER VAN TRAVEL JOURNAL

DATE .... MILEAGE START ....
DEPARTURE TIME .... MILEAGE END ....
ARRIVAL TIME .... MILEAGE TOTAL ....

CAMPSITE NAME ....
ADDRESS 1 ....
ADDRESS 2 ....
POST CODE .... GPS ....
E MAIL .... PHONE ....
WEBSITE WWW...
MY RATING ☆☆☆☆☆☆☆☆   RECOMMEND YES/NO
WEATHER .... TEMPERATURE ....

WILD CAMPING LOCATION/ NOTES

....
....
....
.... GPS ....

DAILY COSTS	TODAY'S HIGHLIGHTS
SITE FEES £ .	....
FUEL £ .	....
LPG GAS £ .	....
TOLLS £ .	....
GROCERIES £ .	....
EATING OUT £ .	....
ENTERTAINMENT £ .	....
OTHER COSTS £ .	....

NOTES

....
....
....
....

CAMPER VAN TRAVEL JOURNAL

DATE .... MILEAGE START ....
DEPARTURE TIME............. MILEAGE END ....
ARRIVAL TIME .... MILEAGE TOTAL ....

CAMPSITE NAME ....
ADDRESS 1 ....
ADDRESS 2 ....
POST CODE .... GPS ....
E MAIL .... PHONE ....
WEBSITE WWW..
MY RATING ☆☆☆☆☆☆☆   RECOMMEND YES/NO
WEATHER .... TEMPERATURE ....

WILD CAMPING LOCATION/ NOTES

....
....
....
....
.... GPS ....

DAILY COSTS		TODAY'S HIGHLIGHTS
SITE FEES	£ .	....
FUEL	£ .	....
LPG GAS	£ .	....
TOLLS	£ .	....
GROCERIES	£ .	....
EATING OUT	£ .	....
ENTERTAINMENT	£ .	....
OTHER COSTS	£ .	....

NOTES

....
....
....
....
....

CAMPER VAN TRAVEL JOURNAL

DATE .... MILEAGE START ....
DEPARTURE TIME .... MILEAGE END ....
ARRIVAL TIME .... MILEAGE TOTAL ....

CAMPSITE NAME ....
ADDRESS 1 ....
ADDRESS 2 ....
POST CODE .... GPS ....
E MAIL .... PHONE ....
WEBSITE WWW..
MY RATING ☆☆☆☆☆☆☆☆   RECOMMEND YES/NO
WEATHER .... TEMPERATURE ....

WILD CAMPING LOCATION/ NOTES

....
....
....
.... GPS ....

DAILY COSTS	TODAY'S HIGHLIGHTS
SITE FEES £ .	....
FUEL £ .	....
LPG GAS £ .	....
TOLLS £ .	....
GROCERIES £ .	....
EATING OUT £ .	....
ENTERTAINMENT £ .	....
OTHER COSTS £ .	....

NOTES

....
....
....
....
....

CAMPER VAN TRAVEL JOURNAL

DATE .... MILEAGE START ....
DEPARTURE TIME............ MILEAGE END ....
ARRIVAL TIME .... MILEAGE TOTAL ....

CAMPSITE NAME ....
ADDRESS 1 ....
ADDRESS 2 ....
POST CODE .... GPS ....
E MAIL .... PHONE ....
WEBSITE WWW...
MY RATING ☆☆☆☆☆☆☆☆☆☆   RECOMMEND YES/NO
WEATHER .... TEMPERATURE ....

WILD CAMPING LOCATION/ NOTES

....
....
....
....
.... GPS ....

DAILY COSTS	TODAY'S HIGHLIGHTS
SITE FEES £ .	....
FUEL £ .	....
LPG GAS £ .	....
TOLLS £ .	....
GROCERIES £ .	....
EATING OUT £ .	....
ENTERTAINMENT £ .	....
OTHER COSTS £ .	....

NOTES

....
....
....
....
....

CAMPER VAN TRAVEL JOURNAL

DATE .... MILEAGE START ....
DEPARTURE TIME............. MILEAGE END ....
ARRIVAL TIME .... MILEAGE TOTAL ....

CAMPSITE NAME ....
ADDRESS 1 ....
ADDRESS 2 ....
POST CODE .... GPS ....
E MAIL .... PHONE ....
WEBSITE WWW..
MY RATING ☆☆☆☆☆☆☆☆   RECOMMEND YES/NO
WEATHER .... TEMPERATURE ....

WILD CAMPING LOCATION/ NOTES

....
....
....
....
............................GPS ....

DAILY COSTS		TODAY'S HIGHLIGHTS
SITE FEES	£ .	....
FUEL	£ .	....
LPG GAS	£ .	....
TOLLS	£ .	....
GROCERIES	£ .	....
EATING OUT	£ .	....
ENTERTAINMENT	£ .	....
OTHER COSTS	£ .	....

NOTES

....
....
....
....
....

CAMPER VAN TRAVEL JOURNAL

DATE .... MILEAGE START ....
DEPARTURE TIME .... MILEAGE END ....
ARRIVAL TIME .... MILEAGE TOTAL ....

CAMPSITE NAME ....
ADDRESS 1 ....
ADDRESS 2 ....
POST CODE .... GPS ....
E MAIL .... PHONE ....
WEBSITE WWW...
MY RATING ☆☆☆☆☆☆☆☆   RECOMMEND YES/NO
WEATHER .... TEMPERATURE ....

WILD CAMPING LOCATION/ NOTES
....
....
....
....
.... GPS ....

DAILY COSTS		TODAY'S HIGHLIGHTS
SITE FEES	£ .	....
FUEL	£ .	....
LPG GAS	£ .	....
TOLLS	£ .	....
GROCERIES	£ .	....
EATING OUT	£ .	....
ENTERTAINMENT	£ .	....
OTHER COSTS	£ .	....

NOTES
....
....
....
....
....

CAMPER VAN TRAVEL JOURNAL

DATE .... MILEAGE START ....
DEPARTURE TIME .... MILEAGE END ....
ARRIVAL TIME .... MILEAGE TOTAL ....

CAMPSITE NAME ....
ADDRESS 1 ....
ADDRESS 2 ....
POST CODE .... GPS ....
E MAIL .... PHONE ....
WEBSITE WWW...
MY RATING ☆☆☆☆☆☆☆☆   RECOMMEND YES/NO
WEATHER .... TEMPERATURE ....

WILD CAMPING LOCATION/ NOTES

....
....
....
....
.... GPS ....

DAILY COSTS		TODAY'S HIGHLIGHTS
SITE FEES	£ .	....
FUEL	£ .	....
LPG GAS	£ .	....
TOLLS	£ .	....
GROCERIES	£ .	....
EATING OUT	£ .	....
ENTERTAINMENT	£ .	....
OTHER COSTS	£ .	....

NOTES

....
....
....
....
....

CAMPER VAN TRAVEL JOURNAL

DATE .... MILEAGE START ....
DEPARTURE TIME .... MILEAGE END ....
ARRIVAL TIME .... MILEAGE TOTAL ....

CAMPSITE NAME ....
ADDRESS 1 ....
ADDRESS 2 ....
POST CODE .... GPS ....
E MAIL .... PHONE ....
WEBSITE WWW..
MY RATING ☆☆☆☆☆☆☆   RECOMMEND YES/NO
WEATHER .... TEMPERATURE ....

WILD CAMPING LOCATION/ NOTES

....
....
....
....
.... GPS ....

DAILY COSTS	TODAY'S HIGHLIGHTS
SITE FEES £ .	....
FUEL £ .	....
LPG GAS £ .	....
TOLLS £ .	....
GROCERIES £ .	....
EATING OUT £ .	....
ENTERTAINMENT £ .	....
OTHER COSTS £ .	....

NOTES

....
....
....
....
....

CAMPER VAN TRAVEL JOURNAL

DATE .... MILEAGE START ....
DEPARTURE TIME .... MILEAGE END ....
ARRIVAL TIME .... MILEAGE TOTAL ....

CAMPSITE NAME ....
ADDRESS 1 ....
ADDRESS 2 ....
POST CODE .... GPS ....
E MAIL .... PHONE ....
WEBSITE WWW...
MY RATING ☆☆☆☆☆☆☆   RECOMMEND YES/NO
WEATHER .... TEMPERATURE ....

WILD CAMPING LOCATION/ NOTES

....
....
....
....
.... GPS ....

DAILY COSTS	TODAY'S HIGHLIGHTS
SITE FEES £ .	....
FUEL £ .	....
LPG GAS £ .	....
TOLLS £ .	....
GROCERIES £ .	....
EATING OUT £ .	....
ENTERTAINMENT £ .	....
OTHER COSTS £ .	....

NOTES

....
....
....
....
....

CAMPER VAN TRAVEL JOURNAL

DATE .... MILEAGE START ....
DEPARTURE TIME .... MILEAGE END ....
ARRIVAL TIME .... MILEAGE TOTAL ....

CAMPSITE NAME ....
ADDRESS 1 ....
ADDRESS 2 ....
POST CODE .... GPS ....
E MAIL .... PHONE ....
WEBSITE WWW..
MY RATING ☆☆☆☆☆☆☆   RECOMMEND YES/NO
WEATHER .... TEMPERATURE ....

WILD CAMPING LOCATION/ NOTES

....
....
....
....
.... GPS ....

DAILY COSTS   TODAY'S HIGHLIGHTS

SITE FEES   £ .   ...
FUEL   £ .   ...
LPG GAS   £ .   ...
TOLLS   £ .   ...
GROCERIES   £ .   ...
EATING OUT   £ .   ...
ENTERTAINMENT   £ .   ...
OTHER COSTS   £ .   ...

NOTES

....
....
....
....

CAMPER VAN TRAVEL JOURNAL

DATE .... MILEAGE START ....
DEPARTURE TIME .... MILEAGE END ....
ARRIVAL TIME .... MILEAGE TOTAL ....

CAMPSITE NAME ....
ADDRESS 1 ....
ADDRESS 2 ....
POST CODE .... GPS ....
E MAIL .... PHONE ....
WEBSITE WWW..
MY RATING ☆☆☆☆☆☆☆☆   RECOMMEND YES/NO
WEATHER .... TEMPERATURE ....

WILD CAMPING LOCATION/ NOTES

....
....
....
....
.... GPS ....

DAILY COSTS		TODAY'S HIGHLIGHTS
SITE FEES	£ .	....
FUEL	£ .	....
LPG GAS	£ .	....
TOLLS	£ .	....
GROCERIES	£ .	....
EATING OUT	£ .	....
ENTERTAINMENT	£ .	....
OTHER COSTS	£ .	....

NOTES

....
....
....
....
....

CAMPER VAN TRAVEL JOURNAL

DATE .... MILEAGE START ....
DEPARTURE TIME............ MILEAGE END ....
ARRIVAL TIME .... MILEAGE TOTAL ....

CAMPSITE NAME ....
ADDRESS 1 ....
ADDRESS 2 ....
POST CODE .... GPS ....
E MAIL .... PHONE ....
WEBSITE WWW..
MY RATING ☆☆☆☆☆☆☆☆☆   RECOMMEND YES/NO
WEATHER .... TEMPERATURE ....

WILD CAMPING LOCATION/ NOTES

....
....
....
....
.... GPS ....

DAILY COSTS		TODAY'S HIGHLIGHTS
SITE FEES	£ .	....
FUEL	£ .	....
LPG GAS	£ .	....
TOLLS	£ .	....
GROCERIES	£ .	....
EATING OUT	£ .	....
ENTERTAINMENT	£ .	....
OTHER COSTS	£ .	....

NOTES

....
....
....
....
....

CAMPER VAN TRAVEL JOURNAL

DATE .... MILEAGE START ....
DEPARTURE TIME .... MILEAGE END ....
ARRIVAL TIME .... MILEAGE TOTAL ....

CAMPSITE NAME ....
ADDRESS 1 ....
ADDRESS 2 ....
POST CODE .... GPS ....
E MAIL .... PHONE ....
WEBSITE WWW...
MY RATING ☆☆☆☆☆☆☆☆   RECOMMEND YES/NO
WEATHER .... TEMPERATURE ....

WILD CAMPING LOCATION/ NOTES

....
....
....
....
.... GPS ....

DAILY COSTS		TODAY'S HIGHLIGHTS
SITE FEES	£ .	....
FUEL	£ .	....
LPG GAS	£ .	....
TOLLS	£ .	....
GROCERIES	£ .	....
EATING OUT	£ .	....
ENTERTAINMENT	£ .	....
OTHER COSTS	£ .	....

NOTES

....
....
....
....
....

CAMPER VAN TRAVEL JOURNAL

DATE .... MILEAGE START ....
DEPARTURE TIME .... MILEAGE END ....
ARRIVAL TIME .... MILEAGE TOTAL ....

CAMPSITE NAME ....
ADDRESS 1 ....
ADDRESS 2 ....
POST CODE .... GPS ....
E MAIL .... PHONE ....
WEBSITE WWW ....
MY RATING ☆☆☆☆☆☆☆   RECOMMEND YES/NO
WEATHER .... TEMPERATURE ....

WILD CAMPING LOCATION/ NOTES

....
....
....
....
.... GPS ....

DAILY COSTS		TODAY'S HIGHLIGHTS
SITE FEES	£ .	....
FUEL	£ .	....
LPG GAS	£ .	....
TOLLS	£ .	....
GROCERIES	£ .	....
EATING OUT	£ .	....
ENTERTAINMENT	£ .	....
OTHER COSTS	£ .	....

NOTES

....
....
....
....
....

CAMPER VAN TRAVEL JOURNAL

DATE .... MILEAGE START ....
DEPARTURE TIME .... MILEAGE END ....
ARRIVAL TIME .... MILEAGE TOTAL ....

CAMPSITE NAME ....
ADDRESS 1 ....
ADDRESS 2 ....
POST CODE .... GPS ....
E MAIL .... PHONE ....
WEBSITE WWW...
MY RATING ☆☆☆☆☆☆☆   RECOMMEND YES/NO
WEATHER .... TEMPERATURE ....

WILD CAMPING LOCATION/ NOTES

....
....
....
....
.... GPS ....

DAILY COSTS	TODAY'S HIGHLIGHTS
SITE FEES £ .	....
FUEL £ .	....
LPG GAS £ .	....
TOLLS £ .	....
GROCERIES £ .	....
EATING OUT £ .	....
ENTERTAINMENT £ .	....
OTHER COSTS £ .	....

NOTES

....
....
....
....
....

CAMPER VAN TRAVEL JOURNAL

DATE .... MILEAGE START ....
DEPARTURE TIME............ MILEAGE END ....
ARRIVAL TIME .... MILEAGE TOTAL ....

CAMPSITE NAME ....
ADDRESS 1 ....
ADDRESS 2 ....
POST CODE .... GPS ....
E MAIL .... PHONE ....
WEBSITE WWW...
MY RATING ☆☆☆☆☆☆☆   RECOMMEND YES/NO
WEATHER .... TEMPERATURE ....

WILD CAMPING LOCATION/ NOTES
....
....
....
....
.... GPS ....

DAILY COSTS	TODAY'S HIGHLIGHTS
SITE FEES £ .	....
FUEL £ .	....
LPG GAS £ .	....
TOLLS £ .	....
GROCERIES £ .	....
EATING OUT £ .	....
ENTERTAINMENT £ .	....
OTHER COSTS £ .	....

NOTES
....
....
....
....
....

CAMPER VAN TRAVEL JOURNAL

DATE .... MILEAGE START ....
DEPARTURE TIME............ MILEAGE END ....
ARRIVAL TIME   .... MILEAGE TOTAL ....

CAMPSITE NAME ....
ADDRESS 1 ....
ADDRESS 2 ....
POST CODE .... GPS ....
E MAIL .... PHONE ....
WEBSITE WWW..
MY RATING ☆☆☆☆☆☆☆☆   RECOMMEND YES/NO
WEATHER .... TEMPERATURE ....

WILD CAMPING LOCATION/ NOTES

....
....
....
....
.... GPS ....

DAILY COSTS		TODAY'S HIGHLIGHTS
SITE FEES	£ .	....
FUEL	£ .	....
LPG GAS	£ .	....
TOLLS	£ .	....
GROCERIES	£ .	....
EATING OUT	£ .	....
ENTERTAINMENT	£ .	....
OTHER COSTS	£ .	....

NOTES

....
....
....
....
....

CAMPER VAN TRAVEL JOURNAL

DATE .... MILEAGE START ....
DEPARTURE TIME............ MILEAGE END ....
ARRIVAL TIME .... MILEAGE TOTAL ....

CAMPSITE NAME ....
ADDRESS 1 ....
ADDRESS 2 ....
POST CODE .... GPS ....
E MAIL .... PHONE ....
WEBSITE WWW...
MY RATING ☆☆☆☆☆☆☆☆☆☆   RECOMMEND YES/NO
WEATHER .... TEMPERATURE ....

WILD CAMPING LOCATION/ NOTES

....
....
....
....
.... GPS ....

DAILY COSTS		TODAY'S HIGHLIGHTS
SITE FEES	£ .	....
FUEL	£ .	....
LPG GAS	£ .	....
TOLLS	£ .	....
GROCERIES	£ .	....
EATING OUT	£ .	....
ENTERTAINMENT	£ .	....
OTHER COSTS	£ .	....

NOTES

....
....
....
....
....

CAMPER VAN TRAVEL JOURNAL

DATE .... MILEAGE START ....
DEPARTURE TIME .... MILEAGE END ....
ARRIVAL TIME .... MILEAGE TOTAL ....

CAMPSITE NAME ....
ADDRESS 1 ....
ADDRESS 2 ....
POST CODE .... GPS ....
E MAIL .... PHONE ....
WEBSITE WWW...
MY RATING ☆☆☆☆☆☆☆☆   RECOMMEND YES/NO
WEATHER .... TEMPERATURE ....

WILD CAMPING LOCATION/ NOTES

....
....
....
....
.... GPS ....

DAILY COSTS   TODAY'S HIGHLIGHTS

SITE FEES   £ .
                                ....
FUEL   £ .
                                ....
LPG GAS   £ .
                                ....
TOLLS   £ .
                                ....
GROCERIES   £ .
                                ....
EATING OUT   £ .
                                ....
ENTERTAINMENT   £ .
                                ....
OTHER COSTS   £ .
                                ....

NOTES

....
....
....
....

CAMPER VAN TRAVEL JOURNAL

DATE .... MILEAGE START ....
DEPARTURE TIME .... MILEAGE END ....
ARRIVAL TIME .... MILEAGE TOTAL ....

CAMPSITE NAME ....
ADDRESS 1 ....
ADDRESS 2 ....
POST CODE .... GPS ....
E MAIL .... PHONE ....
WEBSITE WWW..
MY RATING ☆☆☆☆☆☆☆☆   RECOMMEND YES/NO
WEATHER .... TEMPERATURE ....

WILD CAMPING LOCATION/ NOTES

....
....
....
....
.... GPS ....

DAILY COSTS	TODAY'S HIGHLIGHTS
SITE FEES £ .	....
FUEL £ .	....
LPG GAS £ .	....
TOLLS £ .	....
GROCERIES £ .	....
EATING OUT £ .	....
ENTERTAINMENT £ .	....
OTHER COSTS £ .	....

NOTES

....
....
....
....
....

CAMPER VAN TRAVEL JOURNAL

DATE .... MILEAGE START ....
DEPARTURE TIME .... MILEAGE END ....
ARRIVAL TIME .... MILEAGE TOTAL ....

CAMPSITE NAME ....
ADDRESS 1 ....
ADDRESS 2 ....
POST CODE .... GPS ....
E MAIL .... PHONE ....
WEBSITE WWW..
MY RATING ☆☆☆☆☆☆☆   RECOMMEND YES/NO
WEATHER .... TEMPERATURE ....

WILD CAMPING LOCATION/ NOTES

....
....
....
.... GPS ....

DAILY COSTS	TODAY'S HIGHLIGHTS
SITE FEES £ .	....
FUEL £ .	....
LPG GAS £ .	....
TOLLS £ .	....
GROCERIES £ .	....
EATING OUT £ .	....
ENTERTAINMENT £ .	....
OTHER COSTS £ .	....

NOTES

....
....
....
....
....

CAMPER VAN TRAVEL JOURNAL

DATE .... MILEAGE START ....
DEPARTURE TIME............. MILEAGE END ....
ARRIVAL TIME .... MILEAGE TOTAL ....

CAMPSITE NAME ....
ADDRESS 1 ....
ADDRESS 2 ....
POST CODE .... GPS ....
E MAIL .... PHONE ....
WEBSITE WWW..
MY RATING ☆☆☆☆☆☆☆   RECOMMEND YES/NO
WEATHER .... TEMPERATURE ....

WILD CAMPING LOCATION/ NOTES

....
....
....
....
.... GPS ....

DAILY COSTS	TODAY'S HIGHLIGHTS
SITE FEES £ .	....
FUEL £ .	....
LPG GAS £ .	....
TOLLS £ .	....
GROCERIES £ .	....
EATING OUT £ .	....
ENTERTAINMENT £ .	....
OTHER COSTS £ .	....

NOTES

....
....
....
....
....

CAMPER VAN TRAVEL JOURNAL

DATE .... MILEAGE START ....
DEPARTURE TIME .... MILEAGE END ....
ARRIVAL TIME .... MILEAGE TOTAL ....

CAMPSITE NAME ....
ADDRESS 1 ....
ADDRESS 2 ....
POST CODE .... GPS ....
E MAIL .... PHONE ....
WEBSITE WWW..
MY RATING ☆☆☆☆☆☆☆☆   RECOMMEND YES/NO
WEATHER .... TEMPERATURE ....

WILD CAMPING LOCATION/ NOTES

....
....
....
....
.................................GPS ....

DAILY COSTS	TODAY'S HIGHLIGHTS
SITE FEES £ .	....
FUEL £ .	....
LPG GAS £ .	....
TOLLS £ .	....
GROCERIES £ .	....
EATING OUT £ .	....
ENTERTAINMENT £ .	....
OTHER COSTS £ .	....

NOTES

....
....
....
....
....

CAMPER VAN TRAVEL JOURNAL

DATE .... MILEAGE START ....
DEPARTURE TIME .... MILEAGE END ....
ARRIVAL TIME .... MILEAGE TOTAL ....

CAMPSITE NAME ....
ADDRESS 1 ....
ADDRESS 2 ....
POST CODE .... GPS ....
E MAIL .... PHONE ....
WEBSITE WWW..
MY RATING ☆☆☆☆☆☆☆☆   RECOMMEND YES/NO
WEATHER .... TEMPERATURE ....

WILD CAMPING LOCATION/ NOTES

....
....
....
....
.... GPS ....

DAILY COSTS	TODAY'S HIGHLIGHTS
SITE FEES £ .	....
FUEL £ .	....
LPG GAS £ .	....
TOLLS £ .	....
GROCERIES £ .	....
EATING OUT £ .	....
ENTERTAINMENT £ .	....
OTHER COSTS £ .	....

NOTES

....
....
....
....
....

CAMPER VAN TRAVEL JOURNAL

DATE .... MILEAGE START ....
DEPARTURE TIME .... MILEAGE END ....
ARRIVAL TIME .... MILEAGE TOTAL ....

CAMPSITE NAME ....
ADDRESS 1 ....
ADDRESS 2 ....
POST CODE .... GPS ....
E MAIL .... PHONE ....
WEBSITE WWW...
MY RATING ☆☆☆☆☆☆☆☆☆   RECOMMEND YES/NO
WEATHER .... TEMPERATURE ....

WILD CAMPING LOCATION/ NOTES

....
....
....
....
.... GPS ....

DAILY COSTS		TODAY'S HIGHLIGHTS
SITE FEES	£ .	....
FUEL	£ .	....
LPG GAS	£ .	....
TOLLS	£ .	....
GROCERIES	£ .	....
EATING OUT	£ .	....
ENTERTAINMENT	£ .	....
OTHER COSTS	£ .	....

NOTES

....
....
....
....
....

CAMPER VAN TRAVEL JOURNAL

DATE .... MILEAGE START ....
DEPARTURE TIME .... MILEAGE END ....
ARRIVAL TIME .... MILEAGE TOTAL ....

CAMPSITE NAME ....
ADDRESS 1 ....
ADDRESS 2 ....
POST CODE .... GPS ....
E MAIL .... PHONE ....
WEBSITE WWW ....
MY RATING ☆☆☆☆☆☆☆☆☆☆   RECOMMEND YES/NO
WEATHER .... TEMPERATURE ....

WILD CAMPING LOCATION/ NOTES

....
....
....
....
.... GPS ....

DAILY COSTS			TODAY'S HIGHLIGHTS
SITE FEES	£	.	....
FUEL	£	.	....
LPG GAS	£	.	....
TOLLS	£	.	....
GROCERIES	£	.	....
EATING OUT	£	.	....
ENTERTAINMENT	£	.	....
OTHER COSTS	£	.	....

NOTES

....
....
....
....
....

CAMPER VAN TRAVEL JOURNAL

DATE .... MILEAGE START ....
DEPARTURE TIME .... MILEAGE END ....
ARRIVAL TIME .... MILEAGE TOTAL ....

CAMPSITE NAME ....
ADDRESS 1 ....
ADDRESS 2 ....
POST CODE .... GPS ....
E MAIL .... PHONE ....
WEBSITE WWW..
MY RATING ☆☆☆☆☆☆☆   RECOMMEND YES/NO
WEATHER .... TEMPERATURE ....

WILD CAMPING LOCATION/ NOTES

....
....
....
.... GPS ....

DAILY COSTS	TODAY'S HIGHLIGHTS
SITE FEES £ .	....
FUEL £ .	....
LPG GAS £ .	....
TOLLS £ .	....
GROCERIES £ .	....
EATING OUT £ .	....
ENTERTAINMENT £ .	....
OTHER COSTS £ .	....

NOTES

....
....
....
....
....

CAMPER VAN TRAVEL JOURNAL

DATE .... MILEAGE START ....
DEPARTURE TIME .... MILEAGE END ....
ARRIVAL TIME .... MILEAGE TOTAL ....

CAMPSITE NAME ....
ADDRESS 1 ....
ADDRESS 2 ....
POST CODE .... GPS ....
E MAIL .... PHONE ....
WEBSITE WWW..
MY RATING ☆☆☆☆☆☆☆   RECOMMEND YES/NO
WEATHER .... TEMPERATURE ....

WILD CAMPING LOCATION/ NOTES

....
....
....
....
.... GPS ....

DAILY COSTS		TODAY'S HIGHLIGHTS
SITE FEES	£ .	....
FUEL	£ .	....
LPG GAS	£ .	....
TOLLS	£ .	....
GROCERIES	£ .	....
EATING OUT	£ .	....
ENTERTAINMENT	£ .	....
OTHER COSTS	£ .	....

NOTES

....
....
....
....
....

CAMPER VAN TRAVEL JOURNAL

DATE .... MILEAGE START ....
DEPARTURE TIME .... MILEAGE END ....
ARRIVAL TIME .... MILEAGE TOTAL ....

CAMPSITE NAME ....
ADDRESS 1 ....
ADDRESS 2 ....
POST CODE .... GPS ....
E MAIL .... PHONE ....
WEBSITE WWW..
MY RATING ☆☆☆☆☆☆☆☆   RECOMMEND YES/NO
WEATHER .... TEMPERATURE ....

WILD CAMPING LOCATION/ NOTES

....
....
....
.... GPS ....

DAILY COSTS   TODAY'S HIGHLIGHTS

SITE FEES   £ .   ...
FUEL   £ .   ...
LPG GAS   £ .   ...
TOLLS   £ .   ...
GROCERIES   £ .   ...
EATING OUT   £ .   ...
ENTERTAINMENT   £ .   ...
OTHER COSTS   £ .   ...

NOTES

....
....
....
....
....

CAMPER VAN TRAVEL JOURNAL

DATE .... MILEAGE START ....
DEPARTURE TIME .... MILEAGE END ....
ARRIVAL TIME .... MILEAGE TOTAL ....

CAMPSITE NAME ....
ADDRESS 1 ....
ADDRESS 2 ....
POST CODE .... GPS ....
E MAIL .... PHONE ....
WEBSITE WWW..
MY RATING ☆☆☆☆☆☆☆☆☆☆   RECOMMEND YES/NO
WEATHER .... TEMPERATURE ....

WILD CAMPING LOCATION/ NOTES

....
....
....
....
.... GPS ....

DAILY COSTS			TODAY'S HIGHLIGHTS
SITE FEES	£	.	....
FUEL	£	.	....
LPG GAS	£	.	....
TOLLS	£	.	....
GROCERIES	£	.	....
EATING OUT	£	.	....
ENTERTAINMENT	£	.	....
OTHER COSTS	£	.	....

NOTES

....
....
....
....
....

CAMPER VAN TRAVEL JOURNAL

DATE .... MILEAGE START ....
DEPARTURE TIME .... MILEAGE END ....
ARRIVAL TIME .... MILEAGE TOTAL ....

CAMPSITE NAME ....
ADDRESS 1 ....
ADDRESS 2 ....
POST CODE .... GPS ....
E MAIL .... PHONE ....
WEBSITE WWW..
MY RATING ☆☆☆☆☆☆☆☆☆ RECOMMEND YES/NO
WEATHER .... TEMPERATURE ....

WILD CAMPING LOCATION/ NOTES
....
....
....
....
.... GPS ....

DAILY COSTS		TODAY'S HIGHLIGHTS
SITE FEES	£ .	....
FUEL	£ .	....
LPG GAS	£ .	....
TOLLS	£ .	....
GROCERIES	£ .	....
EATING OUT	£ .	....
ENTERTAINMENT	£ .	....
OTHER COSTS	£ .	....

NOTES
....
....
....
....
....

CAMPER VAN TRAVEL JOURNAL

DATE .... MILEAGE START ....
DEPARTURE TIME............. MILEAGE END ....
ARRIVAL TIME   .... MILEAGE TOTAL ....

CAMPSITE NAME ....
ADDRESS 1 ....
ADDRESS 2 ....
POST CODE .... GPS ....
E MAIL .... PHONE ....
WEBSITE WWW..
MY RATING ☆☆☆☆☆☆☆☆☆☆   RECOMMEND YES/NO
WEATHER .... TEMPERATURE ....

WILD CAMPING LOCATION/ NOTES

....
....
....
....
.... GPS ....

DAILY COSTS			TODAY'S HIGHLIGHTS
SITE FEES	£	.	....
FUEL	£	.	....
LPG GAS	£	.	....
TOLLS	£	.	....
GROCERIES	£	.	....
EATING OUT	£	.	....
ENTERTAINMENT	£	.	....
OTHER COSTS	£	.	....

NOTES

....
....
....
....
....

CAMPER VAN TRAVEL JOURNAL

DATE .... MILEAGE START ....
DEPARTURE TIME .... MILEAGE END ....
ARRIVAL TIME .... MILEAGE TOTAL ....

CAMPSITE NAME ....
ADDRESS 1 ....
ADDRESS 2 ....
POST CODE .... GPS ....
E MAIL .... PHONE ....
WEBSITE WWW..
MY RATING ☆☆☆☆☆☆☆☆   RECOMMEND YES/NO
WEATHER .... TEMPERATURE ....

WILD CAMPING LOCATION/ NOTES

....
....
....
.... GPS ....

DAILY COSTS		TODAY'S HIGHLIGHTS
SITE FEES	£ .	....
FUEL	£ .	....
LPG GAS	£ .	....
TOLLS	£ .	....
GROCERIES	£ .	....
EATING OUT	£ .	....
ENTERTAINMENT	£ .	....
OTHER COSTS	£ .	....

NOTES

....
....
....
....
....

CAMPER VAN TRAVEL JOURNAL

DATE .... MILEAGE START ....
DEPARTURE TIME .... MILEAGE END ....
ARRIVAL TIME .... MILEAGE TOTAL ....

CAMPSITE NAME ....
ADDRESS 1 ....
ADDRESS 2 ....
POST CODE .... GPS ....
E MAIL .... PHONE ....
WEBSITE WWW ....
MY RATING ☆☆☆☆☆☆☆   RECOMMEND YES/NO
WEATHER .... TEMPERATURE ....

WILD CAMPING LOCATION/ NOTES

....
....
....
....
.... GPS ....

DAILY COSTS	TODAY'S HIGHLIGHTS
SITE FEES £ .	....
FUEL £ .	....
LPG GAS £ .	....
TOLLS £ .	....
GROCERIES £ .	....
EATING OUT £ .	....
ENTERTAINMENT £ .	....
OTHER COSTS £ .	....

NOTES

....
....
....
....
....

CAMPER VAN TRAVEL JOURNAL

DATE .... MILEAGE START ....
DEPARTURE TIME .... MILEAGE END ....
ARRIVAL TIME   .... MILEAGE TOTAL ....

CAMPSITE NAME ....
ADDRESS 1 ....
ADDRESS 2 ....
POST CODE .... GPS ....
E MAIL .... PHONE ....
WEBSITE WWW..
MY RATING ☆☆☆☆☆☆☆☆   RECOMMEND YES/NO
WEATHER .... TEMPERATURE ....

WILD CAMPING LOCATION/ NOTES

....
....
....
....
.... GPS ....

DAILY COSTS		TODAY'S HIGHLIGHTS
SITE FEES	£ .	....
FUEL	£ .	....
LPG GAS	£ .	....
TOLLS	£ .	....
GROCERIES	£ .	....
EATING OUT	£ .	....
ENTERTAINMENT	£ .	....
OTHER COSTS	£ .	....

NOTES

....
....
....
....
....

CAMPER VAN TRAVEL JOURNAL

DATE .... MILEAGE START ....
DEPARTURE TIME .... MILEAGE END ....
ARRIVAL TIME .... MILEAGE TOTAL ....

CAMPSITE NAME ....
ADDRESS 1 ....
ADDRESS 2 ....
POST CODE .... GPS ....
E MAIL .... PHONE ....
WEBSITE WWW...
MY RATING ☆☆☆☆☆☆☆☆☆☆   RECOMMEND YES/NO
WEATHER .... TEMPERATURE ....

WILD CAMPING LOCATION/ NOTES

....
....
....
....
.... GPS ....

DAILY COSTS		TODAY'S HIGHLIGHTS
SITE FEES	£ .	....
FUEL	£ .	....
LPG GAS	£ .	....
TOLLS	£ .	....
GROCERIES	£ .	....
EATING OUT	£ .	....
ENTERTAINMENT	£ .	....
OTHER COSTS	£ .	....

NOTES

....
....
....
....
....

CAMPER VAN TRAVEL JOURNAL

DATE ....   MILEAGE START ....
DEPARTURE TIME ....   MILEAGE END   ....
ARRIVAL TIME   ....   MILEAGE TOTAL ....

CAMPSITE NAME ....
ADDRESS 1 ....
ADDRESS 2 ....
POST CODE ....   GPS ....
E MAIL ....   PHONE ....
WEBSITE WWW...
MY RATING ☆☆☆☆☆☆☆☆   RECOMMEND YES/NO
WEATHER ....   TEMPERATURE ....

WILD CAMPING LOCATION/ NOTES

....
....
....
....
.... GPS ....

DAILY COSTS	TODAY'S HIGHLIGHTS
SITE FEES £ .	....
FUEL £ .	....
LPG GAS £ .	....
TOLLS £ .	....
GROCERIES £ .	....
EATING OUT £ .	....
ENTERTAINMENT £ .	....
OTHER COSTS £ .	....

NOTES

....
....
....
....
....

CAMPER VAN TRAVEL JOURNAL

DATE .... MILEAGE START ....
DEPARTURE TIME............. MILEAGE END ....
ARRIVAL TIME   .... MILEAGE TOTAL ....

CAMPSITE NAME ....
ADDRESS 1 ....
ADDRESS 2 ....
POST CODE .... GPS ....
E MAIL .... PHONE ....
WEBSITE WWW..
MY RATING ☆☆☆☆☆☆☆☆☆   RECOMMEND YES/NO
WEATHER .... TEMPERATURE ....

WILD CAMPING LOCATION/ NOTES

....
....
....
....
.... GPS ....

DAILY COSTS	TODAY'S HIGHLIGHTS
SITE FEES £ .	....
FUEL £ .	....
LPG GAS £ .	....
TOLLS £ .	....
GROCERIES £ .	....
EATING OUT £ .	....
ENTERTAINMENT £ .	....
OTHER COSTS £ .	....

NOTES

....
....
....
....
....

CAMPER VAN TRAVEL JOURNAL

DATE .... MILEAGE START ....
DEPARTURE TIME .... MILEAGE END ....
ARRIVAL TIME .... MILEAGE TOTAL ....

CAMPSITE NAME ....
ADDRESS 1 ....
ADDRESS 2 ....
POST CODE .... GPS ....
E MAIL .... PHONE ....
WEBSITE WWW..
MY RATING ☆☆☆☆☆☆☆   RECOMMEND YES/NO
WEATHER .... TEMPERATURE ....

WILD CAMPING LOCATION/ NOTES

....
....
....
....
.... GPS ....

DAILY COSTS	TODAY'S HIGHLIGHTS
SITE FEES £ .	....
FUEL £ .	....
LPG GAS £ .	....
TOLLS £ .	....
GROCERIES £ .	....
EATING OUT £ .	....
ENTERTAINMENT £ .	....
OTHER COSTS £ .	....

NOTES

....
....
....
....
....

CAMPER VAN TRAVEL JOURNAL

DATE .... MILEAGE START ....
DEPARTURE TIME .... MILEAGE END ....
ARRIVAL TIME .... MILEAGE TOTAL ....

CAMPSITE NAME ....
ADDRESS 1 ....
ADDRESS 2 ....
POST CODE .... GPS ....
E MAIL .... PHONE ....
WEBSITE WWW..
MY RATING ☆☆☆☆☆☆☆   RECOMMEND YES/NO
WEATHER .... TEMPERATURE ....

WILD CAMPING LOCATION/ NOTES

....
....
....
....
.... GPS ....

DAILY COSTS	TODAY'S HIGHLIGHTS
SITE FEES £ .	....
FUEL £ .	....
LPG GAS £ .	....
TOLLS £ .	....
GROCERIES £ .	....
EATING OUT £ .	....
ENTERTAINMENT £ .	....
OTHER COSTS £ .	....

NOTES

....
....
....
....
....

CAMPER VAN TRAVEL JOURNAL

DATE .... MILEAGE START ....
DEPARTURE TIME .... MILEAGE END ....
ARRIVAL TIME .... MILEAGE TOTAL ....

CAMPSITE NAME ....
ADDRESS 1 ....
ADDRESS 2 ....
POST CODE .... GPS ....
E MAIL .... PHONE ....
WEBSITE WWW...
MY RATING ☆☆☆☆☆☆☆☆   RECOMMEND YES/NO
WEATHER .... TEMPERATURE ....

WILD CAMPING LOCATION/ NOTES

....
....
....
.... GPS ....

DAILY COSTS	TODAY'S HIGHLIGHTS
SITE FEES £ .	....
FUEL £ .	....
LPG GAS £ .	....
TOLLS £ .	....
GROCERIES £ .	....
EATING OUT £ .	....
ENTERTAINMENT £ .	....
OTHER COSTS £ .	....

NOTES

....
....
....
....
....

CAMPER VAN TRAVEL JOURNAL

DATE .... MILEAGE START ....
DEPARTURE TIME .... MILEAGE END ....
ARRIVAL TIME .... MILEAGE TOTAL ....

CAMPSITE NAME ....
ADDRESS 1 ....
ADDRESS 2 ....
POST CODE .... GPS ....
E MAIL .... PHONE ....
WEBSITE WWW ....
MY RATING ☆☆☆☆☆☆☆☆☆☆   RECOMMEND YES/NO
WEATHER .... TEMPERATURE ....

WILD CAMPING LOCATION/ NOTES

....
....
....
....
.... GPS ....

DAILY COSTS	TODAY'S HIGHLIGHTS
SITE FEES £ .	....
FUEL £ .	....
LPG GAS £ .	....
TOLLS £ .	....
GROCERIES £ .	....
EATING OUT £ .	....
ENTERTAINMENT £ .	....
OTHER COSTS £ .	....

NOTES

....
....
....
....
....

CAMPER VAN TRAVEL JOURNAL

DATE .... MILEAGE START ....
DEPARTURE TIME .... MILEAGE END ....
ARRIVAL TIME .... MILEAGE TOTAL ....

CAMPSITE NAME ....
ADDRESS 1 ....
ADDRESS 2 ....
POST CODE .... GPS ....
E MAIL .... PHONE ....
WEBSITE WWW. ....
MY RATING ☆☆☆☆☆☆☆☆☆   RECOMMEND YES/NO
WEATHER .... TEMPERATURE ....

WILD CAMPING LOCATION/ NOTES

....
....
....
....
.... GPS ....

DAILY COSTS	TODAY'S HIGHLIGHTS
SITE FEES £ .	....
FUEL £ .	....
LPG GAS £ .	....
TOLLS £ .	....
GROCERIES £ .	....
EATING OUT £ .	....
ENTERTAINMENT £ .	....
OTHER COSTS £ .	....

NOTES

....
....
....
....
....

CAMPER VAN TRAVEL JOURNAL

DATE .... MILEAGE START ....
DEPARTURE TIME .... MILEAGE END ....
ARRIVAL TIME .... MILEAGE TOTAL ....

CAMPSITE NAME ....
ADDRESS 1 ....
ADDRESS 2 ....
POST CODE .... GPS ....
E MAIL .... PHONE ....
WEBSITE WWW..
MY RATING ☆☆☆☆☆☆☆☆   RECOMMEND YES/NO
WEATHER .... TEMPERATURE ....

WILD CAMPING LOCATION/ NOTES

....
....
....
....
.... GPS ....

DAILY COSTS		TODAY'S HIGHLIGHTS
SITE FEES	£ .	....
FUEL	£ .	....
LPG GAS	£ .	....
TOLLS	£ .	....
GROCERIES	£ .	....
EATING OUT	£ .	....
ENTERTAINMENT	£ .	....
OTHER COSTS	£ .	....

NOTES

....
....
....
....
....

CAMPER VAN TRAVEL JOURNAL

DATE .... MILEAGE START ....
DEPARTURE TIME .... MILEAGE END ....
ARRIVAL TIME .... MILEAGE TOTAL ....

CAMPSITE NAME ....
ADDRESS 1 ....
ADDRESS 2 ....
POST CODE .... GPS ....
E MAIL .... PHONE ....
WEBSITE WWW ....
MY RATING ☆☆☆☆☆☆☆☆   RECOMMEND YES/NO
WEATHER .... TEMPERATURE ....

WILD CAMPING LOCATION/ NOTES

....
....
....
....
.... GPS ....

DAILY COSTS		TODAY'S HIGHLIGHTS
SITE FEES	£ .	....
FUEL	£ .	....
LPG GAS	£ .	....
TOLLS	£ .	....
GROCERIES	£ .	....
EATING OUT	£ .	....
ENTERTAINMENT	£ .	....
OTHER COSTS	£ .	....

NOTES

....
....
....
....
....

CAMPER VAN TRAVEL JOURNAL

DATE .... MILEAGE START ....
DEPARTURE TIME .... MILEAGE END ....
ARRIVAL TIME .... MILEAGE TOTAL ....

CAMPSITE NAME ....
ADDRESS 1 ....
ADDRESS 2 ....
POST CODE .... GPS ....
E MAIL .... PHONE ....
WEBSITE WWW...
MY RATING ☆☆☆☆☆☆☆   RECOMMEND YES/NO
WEATHER .... TEMPERATURE ....

WILD CAMPING LOCATION/ NOTES
....
....
....
....
.... GPS ....

DAILY COSTS		TODAY'S HIGHLIGHTS
SITE FEES	£ .	....
FUEL	£ .	....
LPG GAS	£ .	....
TOLLS	£ .	....
GROCERIES	£ .	....
EATING OUT	£ .	....
ENTERTAINMENT	£ .	....
OTHER COSTS	£ .	....

NOTES
....
....
....
....

CAMPER VAN TRAVEL JOURNAL

DATE .... MILEAGE START ....
DEPARTURE TIME .... MILEAGE END ....
ARRIVAL TIME .... MILEAGE TOTAL ....

CAMPSITE NAME ....
ADDRESS 1 ....
ADDRESS 2 ....
POST CODE .... GPS ....
E MAIL .... PHONE ....
WEBSITE WWW..
MY RATING ☆☆☆☆☆☆☆☆   RECOMMEND YES/NO
WEATHER .... TEMPERATURE ....

WILD CAMPING LOCATION/ NOTES

....
....
....
....
.............................GPS ....

DAILY COSTS		TODAY'S HIGHLIGHTS
SITE FEES	£ .	....
FUEL	£ .	....
LPG GAS	£ .	....
TOLLS	£ .	....
GROCERIES	£ .	....
EATING OUT	£ .	....
ENTERTAINMENT	£ .	....
OTHER COSTS	£ .	....

NOTES

....
....
....
....
....

CAMPER VAN TRAVEL JOURNAL

DATE .... MILEAGE START ....
DEPARTURE TIME .... MILEAGE END ....
ARRIVAL TIME .... MILEAGE TOTAL ....

CAMPSITE NAME ....
ADDRESS 1 ....
ADDRESS 2 ....
POST CODE .... GPS ....
E MAIL .... PHONE ....
WEBSITE WWW..
MY RATING ☆☆☆☆☆☆☆☆☆☆   RECOMMEND YES/NO
WEATHER .... TEMPERATURE ....

WILD CAMPING LOCATION/ NOTES

....
....
....
....
.... GPS ....

DAILY COSTS		TODAY'S HIGHLIGHTS
SITE FEES	£ .	....
FUEL	£ .	....
LPG GAS	£ .	....
TOLLS	£ .	....
GROCERIES	£ .	....
EATING OUT	£ .	....
ENTERTAINMENT	£ .	....
OTHER COSTS	£ .	....

NOTES

....
....
....
....
....

CAMPER VAN TRAVEL JOURNAL

DATE .... MILEAGE START ....
DEPARTURE TIME .... MILEAGE END ....
ARRIVAL TIME .... MILEAGE TOTAL ....

CAMPSITE NAME ....
ADDRESS 1 ....
ADDRESS 2 ....
POST CODE .... GPS ....
E MAIL .... PHONE ....
WEBSITE WWW...
MY RATING ☆☆☆☆☆☆☆☆   RECOMMEND YES/NO
WEATHER .... TEMPERATURE ....

WILD CAMPING LOCATION/ NOTES

....
....
....
....GPS ....

DAILY COSTS	TODAY'S HIGHLIGHTS
SITE FEES £ .	....
FUEL £ .	....
LPG GAS £ .	....
TOLLS £ .	....
GROCERIES £ .	....
EATING OUT £ .	....
ENTERTAINMENT £ .	....
OTHER COSTS £ .	....

NOTES

....
....
....
....
....

CAMPER VAN TRAVEL JOURNAL

DATE .... MILEAGE START ....
DEPARTURE TIME .... MILEAGE END ....
ARRIVAL TIME .... MILEAGE TOTAL ....

CAMPSITE NAME ....
ADDRESS 1 ....
ADDRESS 2 ....
POST CODE .... GPS ....
E MAIL .... PHONE ....
WEBSITE WWW..
MY RATING ☆☆☆☆☆☆☆   RECOMMEND YES/NO
WEATHER .... TEMPERATURE ....

WILD CAMPING LOCATION/ NOTES

....
....
....
....
.... GPS ....

DAILY COSTS		TODAY'S HIGHLIGHTS
SITE FEES	£ .	....
FUEL	£ .	....
LPG GAS	£ .	....
TOLLS	£ .	....
GROCERIES	£ .	....
EATING OUT	£ .	....
ENTERTAINMENT	£ .	....
OTHER COSTS	£ .	....

NOTES

....
....
....
....
....

CAMPER VAN TRAVEL JOURNAL

DATE .... MILEAGE START ....
DEPARTURE TIME .... MILEAGE END ....
ARRIVAL TIME .... MILEAGE TOTAL ....

CAMPSITE NAME ....
ADDRESS 1 ....
ADDRESS 2 ....
POST CODE .... GPS ....
E MAIL .... PHONE ....
WEBSITE WWW...
MY RATING ☆☆☆☆☆☆☆   RECOMMEND YES/NO
WEATHER .... TEMPERATURE ....

WILD CAMPING LOCATION/ NOTES

....
....
....
....
.... GPS ....

DAILY COSTS	TODAY'S HIGHLIGHTS
SITE FEES £ .	....
FUEL £ .	....
LPG GAS £ .	....
TOLLS £ .	....
GROCERIES £ .	....
EATING OUT £ .	....
ENTERTAINMENT £ .	....
OTHER COSTS £ .	....

NOTES

....
....
....
....
....

CAMPER VAN TRAVEL JOURNAL

DATE .... MILEAGE START ....
DEPARTURE TIME .... MILEAGE END ....
ARRIVAL TIME .... MILEAGE TOTAL ....

CAMPSITE NAME ....
ADDRESS 1 ....
ADDRESS 2 ....
POST CODE .... GPS ....
E MAIL .... PHONE ....
WEBSITE WWW..
MY RATING ☆☆☆☆☆☆☆☆   RECOMMEND YES/NO
WEATHER .... TEMPERATURE ....

WILD CAMPING LOCATION/ NOTES

....
....
....
....
.... GPS ....

DAILY COSTS		TODAY'S HIGHLIGHTS
SITE FEES	£ .	....
FUEL	£ .	....
LPG GAS	£ .	....
TOLLS	£ .	....
GROCERIES	£ .	....
EATING OUT	£ .	....
ENTERTAINMENT	£ .	....
OTHER COSTS	£ .	....

NOTES

....
....
....
....
....

CAMPER VAN TRAVEL JOURNAL

DATE .... MILEAGE START ....
DEPARTURE TIME .... MILEAGE END ....
ARRIVAL TIME .... MILEAGE TOTAL ....

CAMPSITE NAME ....
ADDRESS 1 ....
ADDRESS 2 ....
POST CODE .... GPS ....
E MAIL .... PHONE ....
WEBSITE WWW..
MY RATING ☆☆☆☆☆☆☆☆   RECOMMEND YES/NO
WEATHER .... TEMPERATURE ....

WILD CAMPING LOCATION/ NOTES

....
....
....
....
.... GPS ....

DAILY COSTS		TODAY'S HIGHLIGHTS
SITE FEES	£ .	....
FUEL	£ .	....
LPG GAS	£ .	....
TOLLS	£ .	....
GROCERIES	£ .	....
EATING OUT	£ .	....
ENTERTAINMENT	£ .	....
OTHER COSTS	£ .	....

NOTES

....
....
....
....
....

CAMPER VAN TRAVEL JOURNAL

DATE .... MILEAGE START ....
DEPARTURE TIME .... MILEAGE END ....
ARRIVAL TIME .... MILEAGE TOTAL ....

CAMPSITE NAME ....
ADDRESS 1 ....
ADDRESS 2 ....
POST CODE .... GPS ....
E MAIL .... PHONE ....
WEBSITE WWW..
MY RATING ☆☆☆☆☆☆☆☆☆☆   RECOMMEND YES/NO
WEATHER .... TEMPERATURE ....

WILD CAMPING LOCATION/ NOTES

....
....
....
....
.... GPS ....

DAILY COSTS			TODAY'S HIGHLIGHTS
SITE FEES	£	.	....
FUEL	£	.	....
LPG GAS	£	.	....
TOLLS	£	.	....
GROCERIES	£	.	....
EATING OUT	£	.	....
ENTERTAINMENT	£	.	....
OTHER COSTS	£	.	....

NOTES

....
....
....
....

CAMPER VAN TRAVEL JOURNAL

DATE .... MILEAGE START ....
DEPARTURE TIME .... MILEAGE END ....
ARRIVAL TIME .... MILEAGE TOTAL ....

CAMPSITE NAME ....
ADDRESS 1 ....
ADDRESS 2 ....
POST CODE .... GPS ....
E MAIL .... PHONE ....
WEBSITE WWW ....
MY RATING ☆☆☆☆☆☆☆☆   RECOMMEND YES/NO
WEATHER .... TEMPERATURE ....

WILD CAMPING LOCATION/ NOTES

....
....
....
....
.... GPS ....

DAILY COSTS	TODAY'S HIGHLIGHTS
SITE FEES £ .	....
FUEL £ .	....
LPG GAS £ .	....
TOLLS £ .	....
GROCERIES £ .	....
EATING OUT £ .	....
ENTERTAINMENT £ .	....
OTHER COSTS £ .	....

NOTES

....
....
....
....
....

CAMPER VAN TRAVEL JOURNAL

DATE .... MILEAGE START ....
DEPARTURE TIME .... MILEAGE END ....
ARRIVAL TIME .... MILEAGE TOTAL ....

CAMPSITE NAME ....
ADDRESS 1 ....
ADDRESS 2 ....
POST CODE .... GPS ....
E MAIL .... PHONE ....
WEBSITE WWW..
MY RATING ☆☆☆☆☆☆☆   RECOMMEND YES/NO
WEATHER .... TEMPERATURE ....

WILD CAMPING LOCATION/ NOTES

....
....
....
.... GPS ....

DAILY COSTS		TODAY'S HIGHLIGHTS
SITE FEES	£ .	....
FUEL	£ .	....
LPG GAS	£ .	....
TOLLS	£ .	....
GROCERIES	£ .	....
EATING OUT	£ .	....
ENTERTAINMENT	£ .	....
OTHER COSTS	£ .	....

NOTES

....
....
....
....
....

CAMPER VAN TRAVEL JOURNAL

DATE .... MILEAGE START ....
DEPARTURE TIME .... MILEAGE END ....
ARRIVAL TIME .... MILEAGE TOTAL ....

CAMPSITE NAME ....
ADDRESS 1 ....
ADDRESS 2 ....
POST CODE .... GPS ....
E MAIL .... PHONE ....
WEBSITE WWW...
MY RATING ☆☆☆☆☆☆☆☆   RECOMMEND YES/NO
WEATHER .... TEMPERATURE ....

WILD CAMPING LOCATION/ NOTES

....
....
....
....
.... GPS ....

DAILY COSTS		TODAY'S HIGHLIGHTS
SITE FEES	£ .	....
FUEL	£ .	....
LPG GAS	£ .	....
TOLLS	£ .	....
GROCERIES	£ .	....
EATING OUT	£ .	....
ENTERTAINMENT	£ .	....
OTHER COSTS	£ .	....

NOTES

....
....
....
....
....

CAMPER VAN TRAVEL JOURNAL

DATE .... MILEAGE START ....
DEPARTURE TIME .... MILEAGE END ....
ARRIVAL TIME .... MILEAGE TOTAL ....

CAMPSITE NAME ....
ADDRESS 1 ....
ADDRESS 2 ....
POST CODE .... GPS ....
E MAIL .... PHONE ....
WEBSITE WWW..
MY RATING ☆☆☆☆☆☆☆   RECOMMEND YES/NO
WEATHER .... TEMPERATURE ....

WILD CAMPING LOCATION/ NOTES

....
....
....
....
.... GPS ....

DAILY COSTS	TODAY'S HIGHLIGHTS
SITE FEES £ .	....
FUEL £ .	....
LPG GAS £ .	....
TOLLS £ .	....
GROCERIES £ .	....
EATING OUT £ .	....
ENTERTAINMENT £ .	....
OTHER COSTS £ .	....

NOTES

....
....
....
....
....

CAMPER VAN TRAVEL JOURNAL

DATE .... MILEAGE START ....
DEPARTURE TIME .... MILEAGE END ....
ARRIVAL TIME .... MILEAGE TOTAL ....

CAMPSITE NAME ....
ADDRESS 1 ....
ADDRESS 2 ....
POST CODE .... GPS ....
E MAIL .... PHONE ....
WEBSITE WWW..
MY RATING ☆☆☆☆☆☆☆☆   RECOMMEND YES/NO
WEATHER .... TEMPERATURE ....

WILD CAMPING LOCATION/ NOTES

....
....
....
....
.... GPS ....

DAILY COSTS	TODAY'S HIGHLIGHTS
SITE FEES £ .	....
FUEL £ .	....
LPG GAS £ .	....
TOLLS £ .	....
GROCERIES £ .	....
EATING OUT £ .	....
ENTERTAINMENT £ .	....
OTHER COSTS £ .	....

NOTES

....
....
....
....
....

CAMPER VAN TRAVEL JOURNAL

DATE .... MILEAGE START ....
DEPARTURE TIME .... MILEAGE END ....
ARRIVAL TIME .... MILEAGE TOTAL ....

CAMPSITE NAME ....
ADDRESS 1 ....
ADDRESS 2 ....
POST CODE .... GPS ....
E MAIL .... PHONE ....
WEBSITE WWW..
MY RATING ☆☆☆☆☆☆☆☆   RECOMMEND YES/NO
WEATHER .... TEMPERATURE ....

WILD CAMPING LOCATION/ NOTES

....
....
....
....
.... GPS ....

DAILY COSTS			TODAY'S HIGHLIGHTS
SITE FEES	£	.	....
FUEL	£	.	....
LPG GAS	£	.	....
TOLLS	£	.	....
GROCERIES	£	.	....
EATING OUT	£	.	....
ENTERTAINMENT	£	.	....
OTHER COSTS	£	.	....

NOTES

....
....
....
....

CAMPER VAN TRAVEL JOURNAL

DATE .... MILEAGE START ....
DEPARTURE TIME .... MILEAGE END ....
ARRIVAL TIME .... MILEAGE TOTAL ....

CAMPSITE NAME ....
ADDRESS 1 ....
ADDRESS 2 ....
POST CODE .... GPS ....
E MAIL .... PHONE ....
WEBSITE WWW..
MY RATING ☆☆☆☆☆☆☆☆☆   RECOMMEND YES/NO
WEATHER .... TEMPERATURE ....

WILD CAMPING LOCATION/ NOTES

....
....
....
....
.... GPS ....

DAILY COSTS		TODAY'S HIGHLIGHTS
SITE FEES	£ .	....
FUEL	£ .	....
LPG GAS	£ .	....
TOLLS	£ .	....
GROCERIES	£ .	....
EATING OUT	£ .	....
ENTERTAINMENT	£ .	....
OTHER COSTS	£ .	....

NOTES

....
....
....
....

CAMPER VAN TRAVEL JOURNAL

DATE .... MILEAGE START ....
DEPARTURE TIME .... MILEAGE END ....
ARRIVAL TIME .... MILEAGE TOTAL ....

CAMPSITE NAME ....
ADDRESS 1 ....
ADDRESS 2 ....
POST CODE .... GPS ....
E MAIL .... PHONE ....
WEBSITE WWW...
MY RATING ☆☆☆☆☆☆☆   RECOMMEND YES/NO
WEATHER .... TEMPERATURE ....

WILD CAMPING LOCATION/ NOTES

....
....
....
....
.... GPS ....

DAILY COSTS		TODAY'S HIGHLIGHTS
SITE FEES	£ .	....
FUEL	£ .	....
LPG GAS	£ .	....
TOLLS	£ .	....
GROCERIES	£ .	....
EATING OUT	£ .	....
ENTERTAINMENT	£ .	....
OTHER COSTS	£ .	....

NOTES

....
....
....
....
....

CAMPER VAN TRAVEL JOURNAL

DATE .... MILEAGE START ....
DEPARTURE TIME .... MILEAGE END ....
ARRIVAL TIME .... MILEAGE TOTAL ....

CAMPSITE NAME ....
ADDRESS 1 ....
ADDRESS 2 ....
POST CODE .... GPS ....
E MAIL .... PHONE ....
WEBSITE WWW..
MY RATING ☆☆☆☆☆☆☆   RECOMMEND YES/NO
WEATHER .... TEMPERATURE ....

WILD CAMPING LOCATION/ NOTES

....
....
....
....
.... GPS ....

DAILY COSTS		TODAY'S HIGHLIGHTS
SITE FEES	£ .	....
FUEL	£ .	....
LPG GAS	£ .	....
TOLLS	£ .	....
GROCERIES	£ .	....
EATING OUT	£ .	....
ENTERTAINMENT	£ .	....
OTHER COSTS	£ .	....

NOTES

....
....
....
....
....

CAMPER VAN TRAVEL JOURNAL

DATE .... MILEAGE START ....
DEPARTURE TIME .... MILEAGE END ....
ARRIVAL TIME .... MILEAGE TOTAL ....

CAMPSITE NAME ....
ADDRESS 1 ....
ADDRESS 2 ....
POST CODE .... GPS ....
E MAIL .... PHONE ....
WEBSITE WWW...
MY RATING ☆☆☆☆☆☆☆☆   RECOMMEND YES/NO
WEATHER .... TEMPERATURE ....

WILD CAMPING LOCATION/ NOTES

....
....
....
....
.... GPS ....

DAILY COSTS		TODAY'S HIGHLIGHTS
SITE FEES	£ .	....
FUEL	£ .	....
LPG GAS	£ .	....
TOLLS	£ .	....
GROCERIES	£ .	....
EATING OUT	£ .	....
ENTERTAINMENT	£ .	....
OTHER COSTS	£ .	....

NOTES

....
....
....
....

CAMPER VAN TRAVEL JOURNAL

DATE .... MILEAGE START ....
DEPARTURE TIME .... MILEAGE END ....
ARRIVAL TIME .... MILEAGE TOTAL ....

CAMPSITE NAME ....
ADDRESS 1 ....
ADDRESS 2 ....
POST CODE .... GPS ....
E MAIL .... PHONE ....
WEBSITE WWW..
MY RATING ☆☆☆☆☆☆☆   RECOMMEND YES/NO
WEATHER .... TEMPERATURE ....

WILD CAMPING LOCATION/ NOTES

....
....
....
....
.... GPS ....

DAILY COSTS	TODAY'S HIGHLIGHTS
SITE FEES £ .	....
FUEL £ .	....
LPG GAS £ .	....
TOLLS £ .	....
GROCERIES £ .	....
EATING OUT £ .	....
ENTERTAINMENT £ .	....
OTHER COSTS £ .	....

NOTES

....
....
....
....
....

CAMPER VAN TRAVEL JOURNAL

DATE .... MILEAGE START ....
DEPARTURE TIME .... MILEAGE END ....
ARRIVAL TIME .... MILEAGE TOTAL ....

CAMPSITE NAME ....
ADDRESS 1 ....
ADDRESS 2 ....
POST CODE .... GPS ....
E MAIL .... PHONE ....
WEBSITE WWW..
MY RATING ☆ ☆ ☆ ☆ ☆ ☆ ☆   RECOMMEND YES/NO
WEATHER .... TEMPERATURE ....

WILD CAMPING LOCATION/ NOTES

....
....
....
....
.... GPS ....

DAILY COSTS			TODAY'S HIGHLIGHTS
SITE FEES	£	.	....
FUEL	£	.	....
LPG GAS	£	.	....
TOLLS	£	.	....
GROCERIES	£	.	....
EATING OUT	£	.	....
ENTERTAINMENT	£	.	....
OTHER COSTS	£	.	....

NOTES

....
....
....
....
....

CAMPER VAN TRAVEL JOURNAL

DATE .... MILEAGE START ....
DEPARTURE TIME .... MILEAGE END ....
ARRIVAL TIME .... MILEAGE TOTAL ....

CAMPSITE NAME ....
ADDRESS 1 ....
ADDRESS 2 ....
POST CODE .... GPS ....
E MAIL .... PHONE ....
WEBSITE WWW..
MY RATING ☆☆☆☆☆☆☆☆☆   RECOMMEND YES/NO
WEATHER .... TEMPERATURE ....

WILD CAMPING LOCATION/ NOTES

....
....
....
....
.... GPS ....

DAILY COSTS	TODAY'S HIGHLIGHTS
SITE FEES £ .	....
FUEL £ .	....
LPG GAS £ .	....
TOLLS £ .	....
GROCERIES £ .	....
EATING OUT £ .	....
ENTERTAINMENT £ .	....
OTHER COSTS £ .	....

NOTES

....
....
....
....
....

CAMPER VAN TRAVEL JOURNAL

DATE .... MILEAGE START ....
DEPARTURE TIME .... MILEAGE END ....
ARRIVAL TIME .... MILEAGE TOTAL ....

CAMPSITE NAME ....
ADDRESS 1 ....
ADDRESS 2 ....
POST CODE .... GPS ....
E MAIL .... PHONE ....
WEBSITE WWW ....
MY RATING ☆☆☆☆☆☆☆☆   RECOMMEND YES/NO
WEATHER .... TEMPERATURE ....

WILD CAMPING LOCATION/ NOTES

....
....
....
....
.... GPS ....

DAILY COSTS	TODAY'S HIGHLIGHTS
SITE FEES £ .	....
FUEL £ .	....
LPG GAS £ .	....
TOLLS £ .	....
GROCERIES £ .	....
EATING OUT £ .	....
ENTERTAINMENT £ .	....
OTHER COSTS £ .	....

NOTES

....
....
....
....
....

CAMPER VAN TRAVEL JOURNAL

DATE .... MILEAGE START ....
DEPARTURE TIME .... MILEAGE END   ....
ARRIVAL TIME   .... MILEAGE TOTAL ....

CAMPSITE NAME ....
ADDRESS 1 ....
ADDRESS 2 ....
POST CODE .... GPS ....
E MAIL .... PHONE ....
WEBSITE WWW..
MY RATING ☆☆☆☆☆☆☆   RECOMMEND YES/NO
WEATHER .... TEMPERATURE ....

WILD CAMPING LOCATION/ NOTES

....
....
....
....
.... GPS ....

DAILY COSTS	TODAY'S HIGHLIGHTS
SITE FEES £ .	....
FUEL £ .	....
LPG GAS £ .	....
TOLLS £ .	....
GROCERIES £ .	....
EATING OUT £ .	....
ENTERTAINMENT £ .	....
OTHER COSTS £ .	....

NOTES

....
....
....
....

CAMPER VAN TRAVEL JOURNAL

DATE .... MILEAGE START ....
DEPARTURE TIME .... MILEAGE END ....
ARRIVAL TIME .... MILEAGE TOTAL ....

CAMPSITE NAME ....
ADDRESS 1 ....
ADDRESS 2 ....
POST CODE .... GPS ....
E MAIL .... PHONE ....
WEBSITE WWW..
MY RATING ☆☆☆☆☆☆☆☆   RECOMMEND YES/NO
WEATHER .... TEMPERATURE ....

WILD CAMPING LOCATION/ NOTES

....
....
....
....
.... GPS ....

DAILY COSTS		TODAY'S HIGHLIGHTS
SITE FEES	£ .	....
FUEL	£ .	....
LPG GAS	£ .	....
TOLLS	£ .	....
GROCERIES	£ .	....
EATING OUT	£ .	....
ENTERTAINMENT	£ .	....
OTHER COSTS	£ .	....

NOTES

....
....
....
....
....

CAMPER VAN TRAVEL JOURNAL

DATE .... MILEAGE START ....
DEPARTURE TIME .... MILEAGE END ....
ARRIVAL TIME .... MILEAGE TOTAL ....

CAMPSITE NAME ....
ADDRESS 1 ....
ADDRESS 2 ....
POST CODE .... GPS ....
E MAIL .... PHONE ....
WEBSITE WWW..
MY RATING ☆☆☆☆☆☆☆   RECOMMEND YES/NO
WEATHER .... TEMPERATURE ....

WILD CAMPING LOCATION/ NOTES

....
....
....
....
.... GPS ....

DAILY COSTS	TODAY'S HIGHLIGHTS
SITE FEES £ .	....
FUEL £ .	....
LPG GAS £ .	....
TOLLS £ .	....
GROCERIES £ .	....
EATING OUT £ .	....
ENTERTAINMENT £ .	....
OTHER COSTS £ .	....

NOTES

....
....
....
....
....

CAMPER VAN TRAVEL JOURNAL

DATE .... MILEAGE START ....
DEPARTURE TIME .... MILEAGE END ....
ARRIVAL TIME .... MILEAGE TOTAL ....

CAMPSITE NAME ....
ADDRESS 1 ....
ADDRESS 2 ....
POST CODE .... GPS ....
E MAIL .... PHONE ....
WEBSITE WWW..
MY RATING ☆☆☆☆☆☆☆ RECOMMEND YES/NO
WEATHER .... TEMPERATURE ....

WILD CAMPING LOCATION/ NOTES

....
....
....
....
.... GPS ....

DAILY COSTS	TODAY'S HIGHLIGHTS
SITE FEES £ .	....
FUEL £ .	....
LPG GAS £ .	....
TOLLS £ .	....
GROCERIES £ .	....
EATING OUT £ .	....
ENTERTAINMENT £ .	....
OTHER COSTS £ .	....

NOTES

....
....
....
....
....

CAMPER VAN TRAVEL JOURNAL

DATE .... MILEAGE START ....
DEPARTURE TIME .... MILEAGE END ....
ARRIVAL TIME .... MILEAGE TOTAL ....

CAMPSITE NAME ....
ADDRESS 1 ....
ADDRESS 2 ....
POST CODE .... GPS ....
E MAIL .... PHONE ....
WEBSITE WWW..
MY RATING ☆ ☆ ☆ ☆ ☆ ☆ ☆ ☆   RECOMMEND YES/NO
WEATHER .... TEMPERATURE ....

WILD CAMPING LOCATION/ NOTES

....
....
....
....
.... GPS ....

DAILY COSTS	TODAY'S HIGHLIGHTS
SITE FEES £ .	....
FUEL £ .	....
LPG GAS £ .	....
TOLLS £ .	....
GROCERIES £ .	....
EATING OUT £ .	....
ENTERTAINMENT £ .	....
OTHER COSTS £ .	....

NOTES

....
....
....
....
....

CAMPER VAN TRAVEL JOURNAL

DATE .... MILEAGE START ....
DEPARTURE TIME .... MILEAGE END ....
ARRIVAL TIME .... MILEAGE TOTAL ....

CAMPSITE NAME ....
ADDRESS 1 ....
ADDRESS 2 ....
POST CODE .... GPS ....
E MAIL .... PHONE ....
WEBSITE WWW ....
MY RATING ☆☆☆☆☆☆☆☆   RECOMMEND YES/NO
WEATHER .... TEMPERATURE ....

WILD CAMPING LOCATION/ NOTES

....
....
....
....
.... GPS ....

DAILY COSTS		TODAY'S HIGHLIGHTS
SITE FEES	£ .	....
FUEL	£ .	....
LPG GAS	£ .	....
TOLLS	£ .	....
GROCERIES	£ .	....
EATING OUT	£ .	....
ENTERTAINMENT	£ .	....
OTHER COSTS	£ .	....

NOTES

....
....
....
....
....
....

CAMPER VAN TRAVEL JOURNAL

DATE .... MILEAGE START ....
DEPARTURE TIME .... MILEAGE END ....
ARRIVAL TIME .... MILEAGE TOTAL ....

CAMPSITE NAME ....
ADDRESS 1 ....
ADDRESS 2 ....
POST CODE .... GPS ....
E MAIL .... PHONE ....
WEBSITE WWW...
MY RATING ☆ ☆ ☆ ☆ ☆ ☆ ☆   RECOMMEND YES/NO
WEATHER .... TEMPERATURE ....

WILD CAMPING LOCATION/ NOTES
....
....
....
....
.... GPS ....

DAILY COSTS	TODAY'S HIGHLIGHTS
SITE FEES £ .	....
FUEL £ .	....
LPG GAS £ .	....
TOLLS £ .	....
GROCERIES £ .	....
EATING OUT £ .	....
ENTERTAINMENT £ .	....
OTHER COSTS £ .	....

NOTES
....
....
....
....
....

CAMPER VAN TRAVEL JOURNAL

DATE .... MILEAGE START ....
DEPARTURE TIME .... MILEAGE END ....
ARRIVAL TIME .... MILEAGE TOTAL ....

CAMPSITE NAME ....
ADDRESS 1 ....
ADDRESS 2 ....
POST CODE .... GPS ....
E MAIL .... PHONE ....
WEBSITE WWW ....
MY RATING ☆☆☆☆☆☆☆   RECOMMEND YES/NO
WEATHER .... TEMPERATURE ....

WILD CAMPING LOCATION/ NOTES

....
....
....
....
.... GPS ....

DAILY COSTS	TODAY'S HIGHLIGHTS
SITE FEES £ .	....
FUEL £ .	....
LPG GAS £ .	....
TOLLS £ .	....
GROCERIES £ .	....
EATING OUT £ .	....
ENTERTAINMENT £ .	....
OTHER COSTS £ .	....

NOTES

....
....
....
....
....

Printed in Great Britain
by Amazon